GW00467652

THE GREAT BIBLE
Discovery

KING DAVID

THE BIBLE IS A BEST-SELLER. IT IS ALSO ONE OF THE MASTER-WORKS OF WORLD LITERATURE - SO IMPORTANT THAT UNIVERSITIES TODAY TEACH 'NON-RELIGIOUS' BIBLE COURSES TO HELP STUDENTS WHO CHOOSE TO STUDY WESTERN LITERATURE.

THE BIBLE POSSESSES AN AMAZING POWER TO FASCINATE YOUNG AND OLD ALIKE.

ONE REASON FOR THIS UNIVERSAL APPEAL IS THAT IT DEALS WITH BASIC HUMAN LONGINGS, EMOTIONS, RELATIONSHIPS, 'ALL THE WORLD IS HERE.' ANOTHER REASON IS THAT SO MUCH OF THE BIBLE CONSISTS OF STORIES. THEY ARE FULL OF MEANING BUT EASY TO REMEMBER.

HERE ARE THOSE STORIES, PRESENTED SIMPLY AND WITH A MINIMUM OF EXPLANATION. WE HAVE LEFT THE TEXT TO SPEAK FOR ITSELF. GIFTED ARTISTS USE THE ACTION-STRIP TECHNIQUE TO BRING THE BIBLE'S DEEP MESSAGE TO READERS OF ALL AGES. THEIR DRAWINGS ARE BASED ON INFORMATION FROM ARCHAEOLOGICAL DISCOVERIES COVERING FIFTEEN CENTURIES.

AN ANCIENT BOOK - PRESENTED FOR THE PEOPLE OF THE SECOND MILLENNIUM. A RELIGIOUS BOOK - PRESENTED FREE FROM THE INTERPRETATION OF ANY PARTICULAR CHURCH. A UNIVERSAL BOOK - PRESENTED IN A FORM THAT ALL MAY ENJOY.

OM publishing
CARLISLE, UK

8

When you get to know anybody at all well, you're likely
to find that he or she is - as we say - 'a bit of a mixture.' That
certainly seems true of David.

David was rough and tough. Palestinian shepherds
had to be. Those qualities were useful later when he
faced Goliath, trained a bunch of outlaws until they
became a disciplined team, and led his armies into
battle. One after another, he defeated the kings of the little
kingdoms around him - Ammon, Moab and the rest.

He was also a poet and a musician. He didn't write all the Psalms of
course, and nobody knows what tunes he wrote, but his songs are
still sung, and even used as prayers.

David felt things deeply. Having himself refused a chance to
kill Saul, he ordered the execution of an Ammonite
who claimed to have done so, even though Saul's
death opened up David's path to a throne. He was
intensely loyal, caring for the son of his friend
Jonathan, who might have been a rival for the
throne except that (very fortunately for David)
he was lame.

David had immense personal charm. Jonathan was
devoted to him and he inspired loyalty in his soldiers and
others who worked for him. His old friends stayed with him even
when Absalom's rebellion made it look as if the end had come
for David.

As so often happens, his faults were closely linked with his good
points. Many people would say that the worst things he did were his
adultery with Bathsheba and his murder of her husband. True, most
kings at the time and many since would have had no conscience
about either of these. But David responded quickly to the story
Nathan told him about the rich man taking the poor man's lamb.
His repentance was swift and whole-hearted.

Perhaps it was because he was aware of his own sins that he failed
to check his son Absalom or, later, to punish him. Did all the
soldiers feel bitter when David mourned the death of the prince
who was guilty of treason? Or did some sympathize with the old
king's bitter grief?

For better and for worse, David was the first real king of Israel. The
capital, Jerusalem, was his city. He had a regular army with a
personal bodyguard. Unlike Saul, he had courtiers. What glory for
David! What problems for the nation in later years!

Finally, one more fact about David. Thousands of Jews and
Christians think of him as the ancestor of the messiah.

2 SAMUEL

1 KINGS

PSALMS

KING DAVID

8

First published as *Découvrir la Bible* 1983

First edition © Librairie Larousse 1983

24-volume series adaptation by Mike Jacklin © Knowledge Unlimited 1994
This edition © OM Publishing 1995

01 00 99 98 97 96 95   7 6 5 4 3 2 1

OM Publishing is an imprint of Send the Light Ltd.,
P.O. Box 300, Carlisle, Cumbria CA3 0QS, U.K.

Introductions: Peter Cousins

British Library Cataloguing in Publication Data
A catalogue record for this book is available from the British Library
ISBN 1-85078-212-1

Printed in Singapore by Tien Wah Press (Pte) Ltd.

DAVID
KING OF JERUSALEM

SCENARIO : Etienne DAHLER
DRAWING: Paolo ELEUTERI-SERPIERI

ABIGAIL, STOP WORRYING! WE'LL HEAR SOMETHING SOON.

MASTER! HERE'S A MAN WHO WANTS TO SPEAK TO YOU. HE...

IT'S TAKING SO LONG!

DAVID! DAVID!

ISRAEL HAS BEEN WIPED OUT! MANY MEN HAVE BEEN KILLED. SAUL AND HIS SON JONATHAN ARE DEAD!

I'VE ESCAPED FROM THE BATTLEFIELD!

WHAT HAPPENED? TELL ME QUICKLY!

THAT'S OUR BROTHER, ASAHEL!

ABNER WAS THE STRONGER.

JOAB! LET'S STOP KILLING ONE ANOTHER! TODAY YOU'RE MOURNING FOR ASAHEL; WHAT WILL HAPPEN TOMORROW?

IN THE MEANTIME, ABNER WAS GATHERING HIS TROOPS ON THE TOP OF THE HILL.

LET'S GO BACK TO HEBRON.

THE WAR BETWEEN THE PEOPLE LOYAL TO SAUL AND DAVID'S FORCES LASTED A LONG TIME, BUT AS TIME PASSED, DAVID BECAME STRONGER AND STRONGER.

SOON ISRAEL WILL FALL INTO MY HAND LIKE RIPE FRUIT, AND ALL THE LORD'S CHILDREN WILL BE UNITED AGAIN.

KING OF ISRAEL, I SALUTE YOU!

YOU WORK QUICKLY, ABNER!

NO, DAVID. ALL THE LEADERS OF ISRAEL ARE JOINING YOU.

TOMORROW I'LL CALL ALL THE TRIBES TOGETHER, SO THAT YOU CAN BE ANOINTED AS SOON AS POSSIBLE.

VERY WELL! GO IN PEACE!

THE NEXT DAY JOAB CAME BACK FROM A RAID AND HEARD ABOUT ABNER'S VISIT. HE WENT STRAIGHT TO DAVID.

AND YOU LET HIM GO? HE CAME TO TRICK YOU! THROW HIM INTO PRISON!

JOAB, I KNOW WHAT I'M DOING.

BRING ABNER BACK. TELL HIM DAVID WANTS HIM.

ABNER WAS BURIED AT HEBRON, AND DAVID ORDERED ALL THE PEOPLE TO MOURN AND FAST FOR A DAY.

TO AVENGE ABNER'S DEATH, TWO MEN MURDERED ISHBOSHETH.

LET'S TAKE HIS HEAD TO DAVID.

THAT SHOULD EARN US A GOOD REWARD!

BUT DAVID WEPT FOR SAUL'S SON, AND HAD THE TWO MURDERERS HANGED.

AFTER THAT THERE WAS NOTHING TO STOP DAVID BECOMING KING OVER THE WHOLE NATION. ALL THE TRIBES WENT TO HEBRON AND ANOINTED HIM KING OF ISRAEL.

DAVID, YOU'VE BEEN ANOINTED. YOU'RE BLESSED BY GOD.

MAY HE GIVE ME THE STRENGTH TO SERVE HIM.

FROM ALL OVER THE LAND THEY BROUGHT CAKES, FIGS, RAISINS, WINE, OIL, AND MANY CATTLE AND SHEEP, TO CELEBRATE.

15

NO ONE IN JERUSALEM WAS ILL-TREATED, NOR WAS THE TOWN SACKED.

YOUR GOD IS MUCH STRONGER THAN THE GODS OF CANAAN!

DAVID FORTIFIED THE TOWN ON ALL SIDES, AND HAD A HOUSE BUILT FOR HIMSELF.

THE CARPENTERS AND STONEMASONS SENT BY THE KING OF TYRE HAVE ARRIVED.

BUT THE PHILISTINES WERE UPSET ABOUT DAVID'S VICTORY AND SET OUT TO ATTACK HIM...

THE LORD'S BROKEN THROUGH MY ENEMIES LIKE A FLOOD!

...TWICE THEY WERE BEATEN.

GATES, OPEN UP...

SO THAT THE KING OF GLORY CAN COME IN!

WHO IS THIS KING OF GLORY?

THE COVENANT BOX WAS BROUGHT INTO THE CITY OF DAVID...

THE LORD STRONG AND MIGHTY!

THEN DAVID THREW OFF HIS ROYAL CLOTHES AND DANCED IN FRONT OF THE COVENANT BOX...

MICHAL, DAVID'S WIFE, WATCHED THE PROCESSION COME INTO THE TOWN...

POOR DAVID! HE'S MAKING A FOOL OF HIMSELF, HALF NAKED LIKE THAT! HE'LL LOSE EVERYONE'S RESPECT!

SAUL'S DAUGHTER MICHAL NEVER HAD A CHILD, BECAUSE IN HER HEART SHE SCORNED DAVID...

THROUGH ONE VICTORY AFTER ANOTHER DAVID'S KINGDOM BECAME BIGGER AND BIGGER.

ALL THE POWER — CIVIL, MILITARY, AND RELIGIOUS — WAS IN HIS HANDS.

WE HAVE MANY TRIBES. WE MUST MAKE THEM INTO ONE NATION.

IN THE STRONG PERMANENT ARMY THERE WAS ALSO THE KING'S BODYGUARD OF 30 BRAVE MEN, MANY OF THEM FROM OUTSIDE ISRAEL.

ZADOK AND AHIMELECH, YOU'LL BE PRIESTS, AND YOU'LL REPORT BACK TO ME.

DAVID HAD MANY SONS; ALL OF THEM HELD HIGH POSITIONS IN THE KINGDOM.

IN THIS WAY, NATHAN, EVERYONE'S LINKED TO ME — BY LOVE, OR FEAR, OR INTEREST — AND GOD'S WORK CAN GO FORWARD.

SOME TIME LATER THE AMMONITE KING DIED AND HIS SON HANUN BECAME KING. DAVID SENT MESSAGES OF SYMPATHY TO HIM.

HANUN, DON'T BE FOOLED! THESE MESSENGERS HAVE COME TO SPY ON YOU.

DAVID MADE YOUR FATHER HIS VASSAL, BUT HE'LL WIPE YOU OUT IF HE CAN!

WE'LL SEE ABOUT THAT!

NOTHING MORE WAS NEEDED TO TRIGGER OFF ANOTHER WAR...

THE ARAMAEANS AND THE AMMONITES FLED FROM THE ISRAELITE ARMY COMMANDED BY JOAB.

BUT ANOTHER ALLIANCE WAS GETTING READY TO CHALLENGE DAVID.

THE ARAMAEANS HAVE RALLIED AROUND HADADEZER. THEIR TROOPS ARE MUSTERING NEAR TO HELAM.

SO THEY DIDN'T LEARN THEIR LESSON! WELL, THIS TIME I'LL GO MYSELF.

DAVID CROSSED THE JORDAN, CAME TO HELAM... AND THE ALLIANCE WAS SMASHED.

I ACCEPT YOUR SURRENDER. YOU'LL PAY ME TRIBUTE EVERY YEAR.

SCENARIO: Etienne DAHLER
DRAWING: Paolo ELEUTERI-SERPIERI

NOW IT'S ONLY THE AMMONITES WE HAVE TO BE AFRAID OF! THEY MUST BE DESTROYED!

YOU SEE TO THAT, JOAB. I MUST STAY IN JERUSALEM...

ONE EVENING SOON AFTERWARDS...

THESE SCENTS OF SPRING MAKE ME FEEL DRUNK...

EACH YEAR, IN SPRING, THE KINGS WENT TO WAR.

WHAT A BEAUTIFUL WOMAN!

DAVID FOUND OUT WHO SHE WAS, AND HAD HER BROUGHT TO THE PALACE.

BATHSHEBA, YOUR HUSBAND'S AWAY AT WAR, AND YOUR KING'S THIRSTY FOR LOVE...

SHE DID NOT GO HOME UNTIL THE NEXT MORNING.

MEANWHILE JOAB WAS STILL BESIEGING RABBAH.

THIS IS THE END. IT'S TIME FOR THE FINAL BATTLE.

TELL DAVID WE'RE ONLY WAITING FOR HIM TO COME, BEFORE WE ATTACK THE CITY.

THIS CROWN IS TOO HEAVY FOR YOUR HEAD!

AS SOON AS DAVID ARRIVED, THE CITY WAS TAKEN...

THE CITIZENS OF RABBAH WERE FORCED TO WORK, AND A GREAT DEAL OF BOOTY WAS TAKEN TO JERUSALEM.

..AND THE DEFEATED KING'S CROWN WAS PLACED ON DAVID'S HEAD.

DAVID HEARD A RUMOUR THAT ABSALOM HAD KILLED ALL HIS BROTHERS.

THREE YEARS WENT BY...

JOAB, GO AND BRING ABSALOM BACK TO JERUSALEM!

I THINK ABSALOM WILL BE THE NEXT KING AFTER DAVID!

YOU THINK SO? HE'S BEEN BACK IN JERUSALEM TWO YEARS NOW, AND DAVID STILL WON'T SEE HIM!

IF THERE IS A FAVOURITE, IT'S RATHER YOUNG SOLOMON.

IT'S GOING TO END BADLY! I'VE ONLY ONE WIFE, AND I'VE NOT HAD ALL THESE PROBLEMS!

ABSALOM WANTED AN INTERVIEW WITH HIS FATHER, SO HE SENT FOR JOAB.

HE WON'T COME!

DO WHAT I TELL YOU... AND IN 2 HOURS HE'LL BE HERE!

39

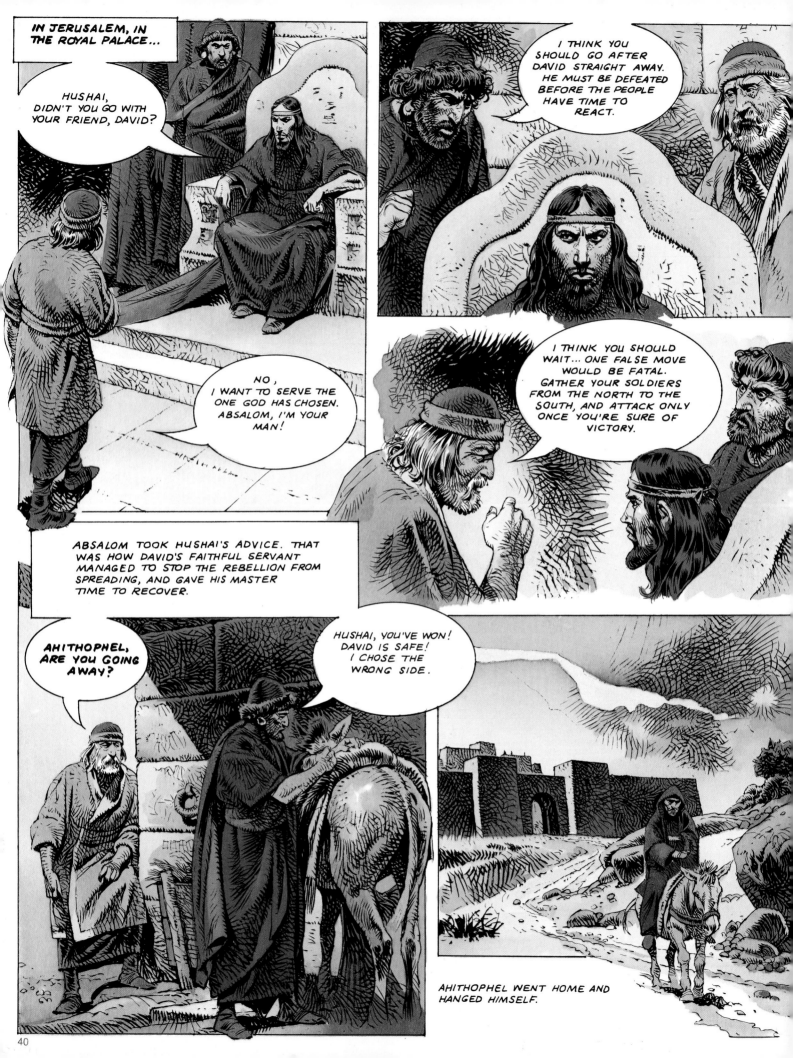

IN JERUSALEM, IN THE ROYAL PALACE...

HUSHAI, DIDN'T YOU GO WITH YOUR FRIEND, DAVID?

NO, I WANT TO SERVE THE ONE GOD HAS CHOSEN. ABSALOM, I'M YOUR MAN!

I THINK YOU SHOULD GO AFTER DAVID STRAIGHT AWAY. HE MUST BE DEFEATED BEFORE THE PEOPLE HAVE TIME TO REACT.

I THINK YOU SHOULD WAIT... ONE FALSE MOVE WOULD BE FATAL. GATHER YOUR SOLDIERS FROM THE NORTH TO THE SOUTH, AND ATTACK ONLY ONCE YOU'RE SURE OF VICTORY.

ABSALOM TOOK HUSHAI'S ADVICE. THAT WAS HOW DAVID'S FAITHFUL SERVANT MANAGED TO STOP THE REBELLION FROM SPREADING, AND GAVE HIS MASTER TIME TO RECOVER.

AHITHOPHEL, ARE YOU GOING AWAY?

HUSHAI, YOU'VE WON! DAVID IS SAFE! I CHOSE THE WRONG SIDE.

AHITHOPHEL WENT HOME AND HANGED HIMSELF.

40

ABIATHAR, TAKE THIS NEWS TO DAVID, AND TELL HIM TO CROSS THE JORDAN AS QUICKLY AS HE CAN.

HUSHAI, I'LL SEND MY SON RIGHT AWAY.

DAVID HURRIED, AND AT DAWN...

...THEY CROSSED THE JORDAN.

SOON THEY REACHED THE TOWN OF MAHANAIM.

SIRE, ACCEPT OUR HOSPITALITY AND OUR HELP.

MEANWHILE ABSALOM, AT THE HEAD OF THE ISRAELITE ARMY, WAS IN PURSUIT, AND WAS ALREADY ACROSS THE JORDAN.

Mediterranean Sea

Jordan

Mahanaim

Gibeon Gilgal

JERUSALEM Jericho AMMONITES Rabbah

AMMON

Hebron Dead Sea

ISHMAELITES

MOABITES

THERE WAS NO WAY OF AVOIDING A BATTLE.

JOAB, FOR MY SAKE DON'T HARM YOUNG ABSALOM!

REMEMBER: DAVID IS THE MAN TO KILL. I DON'T CARE ABOUT THE OTHERS.

ABSALOM, WHERE'S YOUR HELMET?

I DON'T NEED IT! THE FIGHT WILL SOON BE OVER.

THE TWO ARMIES MET IN THE FOREST OF EPHRAIM.

THAT'S ABSALOM!

AFTER HIM!

HEY! THIS WAY! BE QUICK!

THE MULE WENT UNDER A TREE, AND ABSALOM'S HEAD WAS CAUGHT IN THE BRANCHES.

YOU HEARD DAVID'S ORDER. DON'T TOUCH HIM. GO AND TELL JOAB!

JOAB HURRIED TO THE SPOT.

WE MUST FINISH THIS TRAITOR OFF!

BURY HIM IN THE FOREST, AND BLOW THE TRUMPET TO END THE FIGHTING.

KING DAVID! ONE MAN, RUNNING THIS WAY!

IF HE'S ALONE, IT MUST BE GOOD NEWS!

GOOD NEWS! GOD HAS DELIVERED YOU FROM YOUR ENEMIES!

ABSALOM?

MAY WHAT HAPPENED TO HIM HAPPEN TO ALL YOUR ENEMIES!

43

THEN DAVID WENT TO THE ROOM OVER THE GATE OF THE TOWN.

ABSALOM! MY SON! IF ONLY I COULD HAVE DIED INSTEAD OF YOU.

THE DAY OF VICTORY CHANGED INTO A DAY OF MOURNING.

MY SON! WHO'LL GIVE ME BACK MY SON?

JOAB CAME TO DAVID.

YOUR MEN HAVE SAVED YOUR LIFE. IS THIS HOW YOU WELCOME THEM?

IF ABSALOM WERE STILL ALIVE, YOU WOULDN'T CARE IF THE REST OF US HAD DIED IN THE BATTLE!

DAVID, PULL YOURSELF TOGETHER! SPEAK TO YOUR PEOPLE! OTHERWISE BY TOMORROW YOU'LL BE ALL ALONE.

DAVID WAS BACK IN THE ROYAL PALACE IN JERUSALEM.

SHEBA CAN HARM US MORE THAN ABSALOM. THE UNITY OF THE KINGDOM IS IN DANGER. YOU MUST ACT AT ONCE.!

JOAB GATHERED THE BEST MEN IN JUDAH TO HUNT DOWN SHEBA.

HE'S HIDING IN THE VILLAGE OF ABEL BETH MAACAH.

SO THE SIEGE OF THE VILLAGE BEGAN.

JOAB DOES THINGS IN A BIG WAY!

WE'LL NOT BE ABLE TO FIGHT AGAINST HIM.

GIVE US SHEBA, AND WE'LL GO AWAY.

WE'LL THROW HIS HEAD OVER THE WALL!

AND THAT'S WHAT HAPPENED.

JOAB WENT BACK TO JERUSALEM, HIS JOB DONE.

BLOOD IS ALWAYS THE PRICE YOU PAY FOR PEACE!

46

FAMINE STRUCK THE LAND THREE YEARS RUNNING.

THE ANIMALS ARE DYING ONE AFTER ANOTHER...

...AND THE CHILDREN ARE GETTING WEAKER EVERY DAY!

DAVID FASTED AND PRAYED TO GOD.

RETURNING TO THE PALACE, HE CALLED THE PEOPLE OF THE TOWN OF GIBEON.

HOW CAN I MAKE UP FOR THE WRONG SAUL DID TO YOU?

GIVE US SEVEN OF HIS SONS, AND WE'LL HANG THEM.

DAVID AGREED, BUT HE SPARED MEPHIBOSHETH, JONATHAN'S SON.

SAVED! WE'RE SAVED!